Dear Parents,

Welcome to the Scholastic Reader series. We have taken over 80 years of experience with teachers, parents, and children and put it into a program that is designed to match your child's interests and skills.

Level 1—Short sentences and stories made up of words kids can sound out using their phonics skills and words that are important to remember.

Level 2—Longer sentences and stories with words kids need to know and new "big" words that they will want to know.

Level 3—From sentences to paragraphs to longer stories, these books have large "chunks" of texts and are made up of a rich vocabulary.

Level 4—First chapter books with more words and fewer pictures.

It is important that children learn to read well enough to succeed in school and beyond. Here are ideas for reading this book with your child:

- Look at the book together. Encourage your child to read the title and make a prediction about the story.
- Read the book together. Encourage your child to sound out words when appropriate. When your child struggles, you can help by providing the word.
- Encourage your child to retell the story. This is a great way to check for comprehension.
- Have your child take the fluency test on the last page to check progress.

Scholastic Readers are designed to support your child's efforts to learn how to read at every age and every stage. Enjoy helping your child learn to read and love to read.

—Francie Alexander
Chief Education Officer
Scholastic Education

For Daniel
— F.R.
For Sam
— J.D.Z.

Text copyright © 1996 by Fay Robinson.
Illustrations copyright © 1996 by Jean Day Zallinger.
Activities copyright © 2003 Scholastic Inc.
All rights reserved. Published by Scholastic Inc.
SCHOLASTIC, CARTWHEEL BOOKS, and associated logos
are trademarks and/or registered trademarks of Scholastic Inc.

Library of Congress Cataloging-in-Publication Data is available.

ISBN: 0-590-26243-2

10 9 8 7   08 09 10 11 12 13/0
Printed in the U.S.A. 23 • First printing, May 1996

GREAT SNAKES!

by **Fay Robinson**

Illustrated by **Jean Day Zallinger**

Scholastic Reader — Level 2

SCHOLASTIC INC. Cartwheel ·B·O·O·K·S· ®

New York Toronto London Auckland Sydney
Mexico City New Delhi Hong Kong Buenos Aires

Two snakes.

Four snakes.

Six snakes.

Eight.

Every single snake is great!

Snakes with diamonds,

stripes,

and dots.

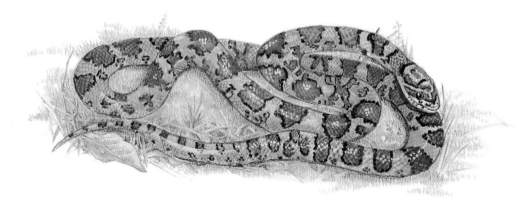

Snakes with many
kinds of spots.

Snakes in deserts.

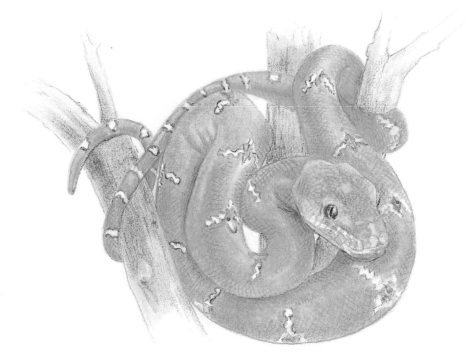

Snakes in trees.

Snakes in mountains.

Snakes in seas.

With no legs,
snakes climb

and slide.

There are snakes
that hang, then glide.

Scaly skin is rough

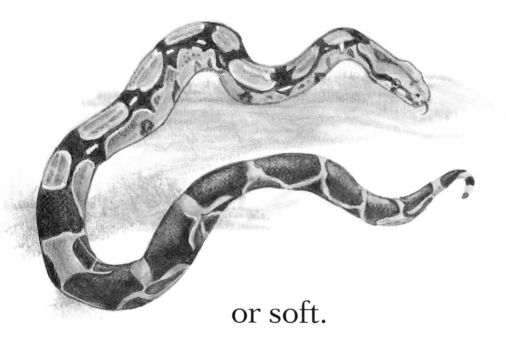

or soft.

When it's old,
it peels right off.

Snakes with fangs—

a scary sight.

Snakes with fangs
have poison bites!

Snakes that
coil small.

Snakes that
stretch tall.

Round and thick snakes.

Thin-like-sticks snakes.

Snakes with flat snouts.

Forked tongues flick out.

Snake eggs.

One snake.

Two snakes.

Three.

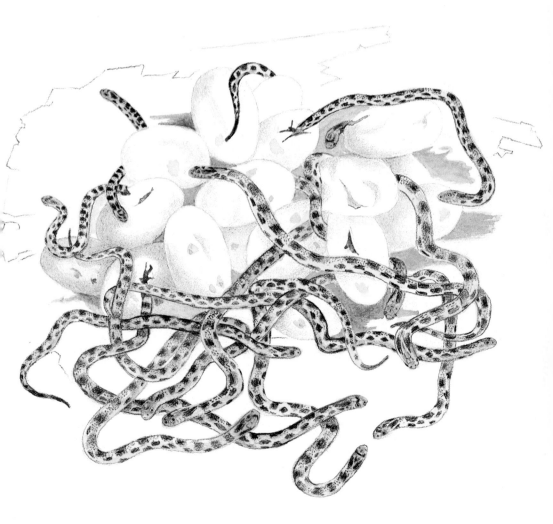

Now how many
do you see?

Snakes eat bugs and
rats and fish.

A lizard makes a
tasty dish.

Chickens, frogs, and,
for a treat, a crocodile—

that's quite a feat!

Snakes with rattles.

Snakes in battles.

Snakes that play dead.

Snakes with two heads.

Two snakes.

Four snakes.

Six snakes.

Eight.
Every single
snake is great!

Cover:
Red Diamond
Rattlesnake

Page 3:
Indian Cobras

Page 4:
Eastern Garter Snake

Page 4:
Red-sided
Garter Snake

Page 4:
Smooth Green Snake

Page 4:
Rosy Boa

Page 5:
Spotted Leaf-nosed
Snake

Page 5:
Sand Snake

Page 5:
Blue Racer

Page 5:
Hognose Snake

Page 6:
Diamondback
Rattlesnake

Page 6:
Coral Snake

Page 7:
Carpet Python

Page 7:
Corn Snake

Page 8:
Saw-scaled Viper

Page 8:
Emerald Tree Boa

Page 9:
Mountain Kingsnake

Page 9:
Banded Sea Krait

Page 10:
Yellow Rat
Snake

Page 10:
Mud Snake

Page 13:
Black Racer

Page 14:
Copperhead Snake

Page 17:
Cottonmouth

Page 17:
Thread Snake

Page 18:
Hognose Snake

Page 11:
Flying Snakes

Page 15:
Gaboon Viper

Page 18:
Python

Page 16:
Pit Viper

Page 12:
Rough-scaled
Tree Viper

Page 12:
Boa Constrictor

Page 16:
Cobra

Page 21:
Fox Snakes

Page 22:
Yellow Rat Snake

Page 23:
Boomslang

Pages 24-25:
Anaconda

Page 26:
Pygmy Rattlesnake

Page 26:
Sand Vipers

Page 27:
Grass Snake

Page 27:
Two-headed
Gopher Snake

Page 28:
Blind Snake

Page 28:
Sonora Whipsnake

Page 28:
Western Ribbon Snake

Page 28:
Kirtland's Water Snake

Page 29:
Common Kingsnake

Page 29:
Ground Snake

Page 29:
Night Snake

Page 29:
Sidewinder